THE

TAMING

OF

THE

SHREW

SHORTENED:

SHAKESPEARE

EDITED

FOR

LENGTH

BY

WILLIAM SHAKESPEARE

EDITED BY

DAVID R. WELLENS, M.A.

THE TAMING OF THE SHREW SHORTENED: SHAKESPEARE EDITED FOR LENGTH

CAST: BAPTISTA -- A RICH GENTLEMAN OF PADUA, VINCENTIO -- AN OLD GENTLEMAN OF PISA, LUCENTIO -- SON TO VINCENTIO (IN LOVE WITH BIANCA), PETRUCHIO -- A GENTLEMAN OF VERONA (SUITER TO KATHERINA), GREMIO -- SUITOR TO BIANCA, HORTENSIO -- SUITOR TO BIANCA, TRANIO -- SERVANT TO LUCENTIO, BIONDELLO -- SERVANT TO LUCENTIO, GRUMIO -- SERVANT TO PETRUCHIO, CURTIS -- SERVANT TO PETRUCHIO, NATHANIEL -- SERVANT TO PETRUCHIO, PETER -- SERVANT TO PETRUCHIO, PEDANT -- SET UP TO IMPERSONATE VINCENTIO, KATHERINA -- THE SHREW (DAUGHTER TO BAPTISTA), BIANCA -- DAUGHTER TO BAPTISTA, WIDOW, TAILOR, HABERDASHER, SERVANTS.

ACT I SCENE III

(Padua.)

(Enter LUCENTIO and his man TRANIO who stand by, BAPTISTA, KATHERINA, BIANCA, GREMIO, HORTENSIO.)

BAPTISTA: Gentlemen, importune me no farther,

For how I firmly am resolv'd you know;

That is, not to bestow my youngest daughter

Before I have a husband for the elder.

If either of you both love Katherina,

Because I know you well and love you well,

Leave shall you have to court her at your pleasure.

GREMIO: To cart her rather; she's too rough for me.

There, there, Hortensio, will you any wife?

KATHERINA: I pray you, sir, is it your will

To make a stale of me amongst these mates?

HORTENSIO: Mates, maid! How mean you that? no mates for you

Unless you were of gentler, milder mold.

KATHERINA: I' faith, sir, you shall never need to fear:

Iwis it is not halfway to her heart;

But if it were, doubt not her care should be

 To comb your noddle with a three-legg'd stool

And paint your face and use you like a fool.

HORTENSIO: From all such divels, good Lord deliver us!

BAPTISTA: Gentlemen, that I may soon make good

What I have said -- Bianca, get you in:

And let it not displease thee, good Bianca,

For I will love thee nere the less, my girl.

KATHERINA: A pretty pet! it is best

Put finger in the eye, an she knew why.

BIANCA: Sister, content you in my discontent.

Sir, to your pleasure humbly I subscribe:

My books and instruments shall be my company,

On them to look and practice by myself.

LUCENTIO: Hark, Tranio! thou mayst hear Minerva speak.

HORTENSIO: Signior Baptista, will you be so strange?

Sorry am I that our good will effects

Bianca's grief.

GREMIO: Why will you mew her up,

Signior Baptista, for this fiend of hell

And make her bear the penance of her tongue?

BAPTISTA: Gentlemen, content ye; I am resolv'd.

Go in, Bianca. *(Exit BIANCA.)*

And for I know she taketh most delight

In music, instruments, and poetry,

Schoolmasters will I keep within my house,

Fit to instruct her youth. *(Exeunt. Remain TRANIO and LUCENTIO.)*

LUCENTIO: Tranio, I burn, I pine, I perish, Tranio,

If I achieve not this young modest girl.

Counsel me, Tranio, for I know thou canst.

Assist me, Trainio, for I know thou wilt.

TRANIO: Master, it is no time to chide you now;

Affection is not rated from the heart:

If love have touch'd you, nought remains but so,

Redime te captam, quam queas minimo.

Thus it stands:

Her elder sister is so curst and shrewd

That till the father rid his hands of her,

Master, your love must live a maid at home;

And therefore has he closely mew'd her up,

Because she will not be annoy'd with suitors.

LUCENTIO: Ah, Tranio, what a cruel father's he!

But art thou not advis'd he took some care

To get her cunning schoolmasters to instruct her?

TRANIO: Ay, marry, am I, sir; and now 'tis plotted.

LUCENTIO: I have it, Tranio.

TRANIO: Master, for my hand,

Both our inventions meet and jump in one.

LUCENTIO: Tell me thine first.

TRANIO: You will be schoolmaster

And undertake the teaching of the maid;

That's your device.

LUCENTIO: It is; may it be done?

TRANIO: Not possible, for who shall bear your part

And be in Padua here Vincentio's son?

Keep house and ply his book, welcome his friends,

Visit his countrymen and banquet them?

LUCENTIO: *Basta,* content thee; for I have it full.

We have not yet been seen in any house

Nor can we be distinguish'd by our faces

For man or master: then, it follows thus:

Thou shalt be master, Tranio, in my stead,

Keep house, and port, and servants, as I should.

I will some other be; some Florentine,

Some Neapolitan, or meaner man of Pisa.

'Tis hatch'd and shall be so: Tranio, at once

Uncase thee, take my color'd hat and cloak.

When Biondello comes he waits on thee;

But I will charm him first to keep his tongue.

TRANIO: So had you need.

In brief, sir, sith it your pleasure is

And I am tied to be obedient --

For so your father charg'd me at our parting:

'Be serviceable to my son,' quoth he,

Although I think 'twas in another sense --

I am content to be Lucentio

Because so well I love Lucentio.

(Exeunt.)

ACT I SCENE IV

(Enter PETRUCHIO, and his man GRUMIO.)

PETRUCHIO: Such wind as scatters young men through the world

To seek their fortunes farther than at home,

Where small experience grows. But in a few,

Signior Hortensio, thus it stands with me:

Antonio, my father, is deceas'd

And I have thrust myself into this maze,

Happily to wive and thrive as best I may.

Crowns in my purse I have and goods at home

And so am come abroad to see the world.

HORTENSIO: Petruchio, shall I then come roundly to thee

And wish thee to a shrewd ill-favor'd wife?

Thou'dst thank me but a little for my counsel

And yet I'll promise thee she shall be rich,

And very rich: but thou'rt too much my friend

And I'll not wish thee to her.

PETRUCHIO: Signior Hortensio, 'twixt such friends as we

Few words suffice; and therefore, if thou know

One rich enough to be Petruchio's wife,

As wealth is burthen of my wooing dance,

Be she as foul as was Florentius's love,

As old as Sibyl, and as curst and shrowd

As Socrates' Zentippe, or a worse,

She moves me not, or not removes, at least,

Affections' edge in me, were she as rough

As are the swelling Adriatic seas.

I come to wife it wealthily in Padua;

If wealthily, then happily in Padua.

HORTENSIO: I can, Petruchio, help thee to a wife

With wealth enough and young and beauteous,

Brought up as best becomes a gentlewoman.

Her only fault -- And that is faults enough --

Is that she is intolerable curst

And shrowd and froward, so beyond all measure,

That were my state far worser than it is

I would not wed her for a mine of gold.

PETRUCHIO: Hortensio, peace! Thou know'st not gold's effect.

Tell me her father's name, and 'tis enough;

For I will board her though she chide as loud

As thunder when the clouds in autumn crack.

HORTENSIO: Her father is Baptista Minola,

An affable and courteous gentleman;

Her name is Katherina Minola,

Renown'd in Padua for her scolding tongue.

PETRUCHIO: I know her father though I know not her,

And he knew my deceased father well.

I will not sleep, Hortensio, till I see her;

And therefore let me be thus bold with you,

To give you over at this first encounter

Unless you will accompany me thither.

GRUMIO: I pray you, sir, let him go while the humor lasts. A my word, and she knew him as

well as I do she would think scolding would do little good upon him.

HORTENSIO: Tarry, Petruchio, I must go with thee

For in Baptista's keep my treasure is.

He hath the jewel of my life in hold,

His youngest daughter, beautiful Bianca,

And her withholds from me and other more,

Suitors to her and rivals in my love,

Supposing it a thing impossible,

For those defects I have before rehears'd,

That ever Katherina will be woo'd.

Therefore this order hath Baptista tane,

That none shall have access unto Bianca

Till Katherine the curst have got a husband.

GRUMIO: Katherine the curst!

A title for a maid of all titles the worst.

HORTENSIO: Now shall my friend Petruchio do me grace

And offer me, disguis'd in sober robes,

To old Baptista as a schoolmaster

Well seen in music, to instruct Bianca,

That so I may, by this device, at least

Have leave and leisure to make love to her

And unsuspected court her by herself.

(Enter TRANIO brave, and BIONDELLO.)

Sir, let me be so bold as ask you,

Did you ever see Baptista's daughter?

TRANIO: No, sir; but heart I do that he hath two,

The one as famous for a scolding tongue

As is the other for beauteous modesty.

PETRUCHIO: Sir, sir, the first's for me; let her go by.

GREMIO: Yea, leave that labor to great Hercules

And let it be more than Alcides' twelve.

PETRUCHIO: Sir, understand you this of me in sooth:

The youngest daughter, whom you hearken for,

Her father keeps from all access of suitors

And will not promise her to any man

Until the elder sister first be wed;

The younger then is free, and not before.

TRANIO: If it be so, sir, that you are the man

Must stead us all, and me amongst the rest;

And if you break the ice and do this feat,

Achieve the elder, set the younger free

For our access, whose hap shall be to have her

Will not so graceless be to be ingrate.

HORTENSIO: Sir, you say well, and well you do conceive;

And since you do profess to be a suitor

You must, as we do, gratify this gentleman

To whom we all rest generally beholding.

TRANIO: Sir, I shall not be slack: in sign whereof,

Please ye we may contrive this afternoon

And quaff carouses to our mistress' health

And do as adversaries do in law,

Strive mightily but eat and drink as friends.

GRUMIO and BIONDELLO: O excellent motion! Fellows, let's be gone.

HORTENSIO: The motion's good indeed, and be it so: --

Petruchio, I shall be your *ben venuto*.   *(Exeunt.)*

ACT II SCENE I

(Enter GREMIO, with LUCENTIO in the habit of a mean man; PETRUCHIO, with HORTENSIO as a musician; and TRANIO, with his boy BIONDELLO bearing a lute and books.)

TRANIO: Toward the education of your daughters

I here bestow a simple instrument,

And this small packet of Greek and Latin books:

If you accept them, then their worth is great.

BAPTISTA: Lucentio is your name, of whence, I pray?

TRANIO: Of Pisa, sir; son to Vincentio.

BAPTISTA: A mighty man of Pisa; by report

I know him well. You are very welcome, sir.

(To HORTENSIO.) **Take you that lute,** *(To LUCENTIO.)* **And you the set of books;**

You shall go see your pupils presently.

Holla, within!

(Enter a SERVANT.)

Sirrah, lead these gentlemen

To my daughters and tell them both

These are their tutors: bid them use them well.

(Exit SERVANT, with LUCENTIO and HORTENSIO, BIONDELLO following.)

You will go walk a little in the orchard

And then to dinner. You are passing welcome

And so I pray you all to think yourselves.

PETRUCHIO: Signior Baptista, my business asketh haste

And every day I cannot come to woo.

You knew my father well, and in him me,

Left solely heir to all his lands and goods,

Which I have better'd rather than decreas'd:

Then tell me, if I get your daughter's love

What dowry shall I have with her to wife?

BAPTISTA: After my death the one half of my lands,

And in possession twenty thousand crowns.

PETRUCHIO: And, for that dowry, I'll assure her of

Her widowhood, be it that she survive me,

In all my lands and leases whatsoever.

Let specialties be therefore drawn between us

That convenants may be kept on either hand.

BAPTISTA: Ay, when the special thing is well obtain'd,

That is, her love; for that is all in all.

PETRUCHIO: Why, that is nothing; for I tell you, father,

I am as peremptory as she proud-minded;

And where two raging fires meet together

They do consume the thing that feeds their fury:

Though little fire grows great with little wind,

Yet extreme gusts will blow out fire and all;

So I to her, and so she yields to me;

For I am rough and woo not like a babe.

BAPTISTA: Well mayst thou woo and happy be thy speed!

But be thou arm'd for some unhappy words.

PETRUCHIO: Ay, to the proof; as mountains are for winds,

That shake not, though they blow perpetually.

(Enter HORTENSIO with his lute's head broke.)

BAPTISTA: How now, my friend! why dost thou look so pale?

HORTENSIO: For fear, I promise you, if I look pale.

BAPTISTA: What, will my daughter prove a good musician?

HORTENSIO: I think she'll sooner prove a soldier.

Iron may hold with her but never lutes.

BAPTISTA: Why, then thou canst not break her to the lute?

HORTENSIO: Why, no; for she hath broke the lute to me.

I did but tell her she mistook her frets

And bow'd her hand to teach her fingering;

When, with a most impatient divelish spirit,

'Frets, call you these?' Quoth she; 'I'll fume with them';

And, with that word, she stroke me on the head,

And through the instrument my pate made way.

PETRUCHIO: Now, by the world, it is a lusty wench!

I love her ten times more than ere I did:

O! how I long to have some chat with her!

BAPTISTA: *(To HORTENSIO.)* Well, go with me, and be not so discomfited.

Proceed in practice with my younger daughter;

She's apt to learn and thankful for good turns.

Signior Petruchio, will you go with us

Or shall I send my daughter Kate to you?

(Exit BAPTISTA, with GREMIO, TRANIO and HORTENSIO. Manet PETRUCHIO.)

PETRUCHIO: I pray you do; I will attend her here

And woo her with some spirit when she comes.

Say that she rail; why then I'll tell her plain

She sings as sweetly as a nightingale;

Say that she frown; I'll say she looks as clear

As morning roses newly wash'd with dew:

Say she be mute and will not speak a word;

Then I'll commend her volubility,

And say she uttereth piercing eloquence.

If she do bid me pack I'll give her thanks

As though she bid me stay by her a week;

If she deny to wed I'll crave the day

When I shall ask the banes, and when be married.

But here she comes; and now, Petruchio, speak.

(Enter KATHERINA.)

Good morrow, Kate; for that's your name, I hear.

KATHERINA: Well have you heard, but something hard of hearing:

They call me Katerina that do talk of me.

PETRUCHIO: You lie, in faith; for you are call'd plain Kate,

And bonny Kate, and sometimes Kate the curst;

But, Kate, the prettiest Kate in Christendom;

Kate or Kate-Hall, my super-dainty Kate,

For dainties are all Kates: and therefore, Kate,

Take this of me, Kate of my consolation:

Hearing thy mildness prais'd in every town,

Thy virtues spoke of, and thy beauty sounded --

Yet not so deeply as to thee belongs --

Myself am mov'd to woo thee for my wife.

KATHERINA: Mov'd! in good time: let him that mov'd you hether.

Remove you hence. I knew you at the first,

You were movable.

PETRUCHIO: Why, what's a movable?

KATHERINA: A joint stool.

PETRUCHIO: Thou hast hit it: come sit on me.

KATHERINA: Asses are made to bear and so are you.

PETRUCHIO: Women are made to bear and so are you.

KATHERINA: No such jade as you, if me you mean.

PETRUCHIO: Alas! good Kate, I will not burthen thee;

For, knowing thee to be but young and light --

KATHERINA: Too light for such a swain as you to catch

And yet as heavy as my weight should be.

PETRUCHIO: Should be! should -- buzz!

KATHERINA: Well tane, and like a buzzard.

PETRUCHIO: O slow-wing'd turtle! shall a buzzard take thee?

KATHERINA: Ay, for a turtle, as he takes a buzzard.

PETRUCHIO: Come, come, you wasp; I' faith you are too angry.

KATHERINA: If I be waspish, best beware my sting.

PETRUCHIO: My remedy is then to pluck it out.

KATHERINA: Ay, if the fool could find it where it lies.

PETRUCHIO: Who knows not where a wasp wear his sting?

In his tail.

KATHERINA: In his tongue.

PETRUCHIO: Whose tongue?

KATHERINA: Yours, if you talk of tales; and so farewell.

PETRUCHIO: What! with my tongue in your tail? nay, come, again.

Good Kate, I am a gentleman.

KATHERINE: That I'll try.

(She strikes him.)

PETRUCHIO: I swear I'll cuff you if you strike again.

KATHERINA: So may you lose your arms:

If you strike me you are no gentleman,

And if no gentleman, why then no arms.

PETRUCHIO: A herald, Kate? O! put me in thy books.

KATHERINA: What is your crest? a coxcomb?

PETRUCHIO: A combless cock, so Kate will be my hen.

KATHERINA: No cock of mine; you crow too like a craven.

PETRUCHIO: Nay, come, Kate, come; you must not look so sour.

KATHERINA: It is my fashion when I see a crab.

PETRUCHIO: Why, here's no crab, and therefore look not sour.

KATHERINA: There is, there is.

PETRUCHIO: Then show it me.

KATHERINA: Had I a glass I would.

PETRUCHIO: What, you mean my face?

KATHERINA: Well aim'd of such a young one.

PETRUCHIO: Now, by Saint George, I am too young for you.

KATHERINA: Yet you are wither'd.

PETRUCHIO: 'Tis with cares.

KATHERINA: I care not.

PETRUCHIO: Nay, hear you, Kate: in sooth you scape not so.

KATHERINA: I chafe you if I tarry: let me go.

PETRUCHIO: No, not a whit: I find you passing gentle.

'Twas told me you were rough and coy and sullen,

And now I find report a very liar;

For thou art pleasant, gamesome, passing courteous,

But slow in speech, yet sweet as springtime flowers.

Thou canst not frown, thou canst not look a sconce,

Nor bite that lip as angry wenches will,

Nor hast thou pleasure to be cross in talk;

But thou with mildness entertain'st thy wooers,

With gentle conference, soft and affable.

Why does the world report that Kate doth limp?

O sland'rous world! Kate, like the hazel-twig

Is straight and slender, and as brown in hue

As hazelnuts and sweeter than the kernels.

O! let me see thee walk: thou dost not halt.

KATHERINA: Go, fool, and whom thou keep'st command.

PETRUCHIO: Did ever Dian so become a grove

As Kate this chamber with her princely gait?

O! be thou Dian and let her be Kate.

And then let Kate be chaste and Dian sportful!

KATHERINA: Where did you study all this goodly speech?

PETRUCHIO: It is extempore, from my mother-wit.

KATHERINE: A witty mother! witless else her son.

PETRUCHIO: Am I not wise?

KATHERINA: Yes; keep you warm.

PETRUCHIO: Marry, so I mean, sweet Katherina, in thy bed;

And therefore, setting all this chat aside,

Thus in plain terms: your father hath consented

That you shall be my wife, your dowry 'greed on;

And will you, nill you, I will marry you.

Now, Kate, I am a husband for your turn;

For, by this light, whereby I see thy beauty --

Thy beauty that doth make me like thee well --

Thou must be married to no man but me.

(Enter BAPTISTA, GREMIO, and TRANIO.)

For I am he am born to tame you, Kate,

And bring you from a wild Kate to a Kate

Conformable as other household Kates.

Here comes your father: never make denial;

I must and will have Katherine to my wife.

BAPTISTA: Now, Signior Petruchio, how spend you with my daughter?

PETRUCHIO: How but well, sir? how but well?

It were impossible I should speed amiss.

BAPTISTA: Why, how now, daughter Katherine! in your dumps.

KATHERINA: Call you me daughter? now, I promise you

You have show'd a tender fatherly regard

To wish me wed to one half lunatic,

A madcap ruffian and a swearing Jack

That thinks with oaths to face the matter out.

PETRUCHIO: Father, 'tis thus: yourself and all the world.

That talk'd of her have talk'd amiss of her.

If she be curst it is for policy,

For she's not froward but modest as the dove,

She is not hot but temperate as the morn;

For patience she will prove a second Grissel

And Roman Lucrece for her chastity;

And to conclude, we have 'greed so well together

That upon Sunday is the wedding day.

KATHERINA: I'll see thee hang'd on Sunday first.

GREMIO: Hark, Petruchio: she says she'll see thee hang'd first.

TRANIO: Is this your speeding? nay, then good night our part!

PETRUCHIO: Be patient, gentlemen, I choose her for myself;

If she and I be pleas'd, what's that to you?

'Tis bargain'd 'twixt us twain, being alone,

That she shall still be curst in company.

I tell you, 'tis incredible to believe

How much she loves me. O! the kindest Kate,

She hung about my neck, and kiss on kiss

She vied so fast, protesting oath on oath,

That in a twink she won me to her love.

O! you are novices; 'tis a world to see

How tame, when men and women are alone,

A meacock wretch can make the curstest shrew.

Give me thy hand, Kate: I will unto Venice

To buy apparel 'gainst the wedding day.

Provide the feast, father, and bid the guests;

I will be sure my Katherine shall be fine.

BAPTISTA: I know not what to say; but give me your hands.

God send you joy, Petruchio! 'tis a match.

GREMIO and TRANIO: Amen, say we: we will be witnesses.

PETRUCHIO: Father, and wife, and gentlemen, adieu.

I will to Venice; Sunday comes apace.

We will have rings and things and fine array;

And, kiss me, Kate, we will be married a' Sunday.

(Exeunt PETRUCHIO and KATHERINE.)

BAPTISTA: Content you, gentlemen; I will compound this strife:

'Tis deeds must win the prize, and he, of both,

That can assure my daughter greatest dower

Shall have my Bianca's love.

Say, Signior Gremio, what can you assure her?

GREMIO: First, as you know, my house within the city

Is richly furnished with plate and gold:

Basins and ewers to lave her dainty hands;

My hangings all of Tyrian tapestry;

In ivory coffers I have stuff'd my crowns;

In cypress chests my arras counterpoints,

Costly apparel, tents, and canopies.

Fine linen, Turkey cushions boss'd with pearl,

Valance of Venice gold in needlework,

Pewter and brass, and all things that belong

To house or housekeeping. Then, at my farm

I have a hundred milch-kine to the pail,

Six score fate oxen standing in my stalls

And all things answerable to this portion.

Myself am strook in years, I must confess;

And if I die tomorrow, this is hers,

If whilst I live she will be only mine.

TRANIO: That 'only' came well in. Sir, list to me:

I am my father's heir and only son,

If I may have your daughter to my wife

I'll leave her houses three or four as good,

Within rich Pisa walls, as any one

Old Signior Gremio has in Padua;

Besides two thousand ducats by the year

Of fruitful land, all which shall be her jointer.

BAPTISTA: Well, gentlemen,

I am thus resolv'd. On Sunday next, you know,

My daughter Katherine is to be married:

Now, on the Sunday following, shall Bianca

Be bride to you if you make this assurance;

If not, to Signior Gremio:

And so I take my leave and thank you both.

(Exit.)

GREMIO: Adieu, good neighbor. Now I fear thee not:

Sirrah young gamester, your father were a fool

To give thee all and in his waning age

Set foot under thy table. Tut! a toy!

An old Italian fox is not so kind, my boy. *(Exit.)*

TRANIO: A vengeance on your crafty wither'd hide!

Yet I have fac'd it with a card of ten.

'Tis in my head to do my master good:

I see no reason, but suppos'd Lucentio

Must get a father, called 'suppos'd Vincentio';

And that's a wonder: fathers commonly

Do get their children, but in this case of wooing

A child shall get a sire if I fail not of my cunning.

(Exit.)

ACT III SCENE II

(Enter BAPTISTA, GREMIO, TRANIO, KATHERINE, BIANCA, LUCENTIO and OTHERS, ATTENDANTS.)

BAPTISTA: *(To TRANIO.)* Signior Lucentio, this is the 'pointed day

That Katherine and Petruchio should be married,

And yet we hear not of our son-in-law.

(Enter PETRUCHIO and GRUMIO.)

PETRUCHIO: Come, where be these gallants? who is at home?

BAPTISTA: You are welcome, sir.

PETRUCHIO: And yet I come not well.

BAPTISTA: And yet you halt not.

TRANIO: Not so well apparell'd

As I wish you were.

PETRUCHIO: Were it better, I should rush in thus.

But where is Kate? where is my lovely bride?

How does my father? Gentles, methinks you frown.

And wherefore gaze this goodly company

As if they saw some wondrous monument,

Some comet, or unusual prodigy?

BAPTISTA: Why, sir, you know this is your wedding day.

First were we sad, fearing you would not come;

Now sadder that you come so unprovided.

TRANIO: And tell us what occasion of import

Hath all so long detain'd you from your wife

And sent you hither so unlike yourself?

PETRUCHIO: Tedious it were to tell and harsh to hear.

Sufficeth, I am come to keep my word

Though in some part enforced to digress;

Which, at more leisure, I will so excuse

As you shall well be satisfied with all.

But where is Kate? I stay too long from her;

The morning wears, 'tis time we were at church.

TRANIO: See not your bride in these unreverent robes.

Go to my chamber; put on clothes of mine.

PETRUCHIO: Not I, believe me; thus I'll visit her.

BAPTISTA: But thus, I trust, you will not marry her.

PETRUCHIO: Good sooth, even thus; therefore ha' done with words:

To me she's married, not unto my clothes.

Could I repair what she will wear in me

As I can change these poor acouterments,

'Twere well for Kate and better for myself.

But what a fool am I to chat with you

When I should bid good morrow to my bride

And seal the title with a lovely kiss! *(Exit with GRUMIO.)*

(Enter GREMIO.)

TRANIO: Signior Gremio, came you from the church?

GREMIO: As willingly as ere I came from school.

TRANIO: And is the bride and bridegroom coming home?

GREMIO: A bridegroom say you? 'Tis a groom indeed,

A grumbling groom, and that the girl shall find.

TRANIO: Curster than she? why, 'tis impossible.

GREMIO: Why, he's a devil, a devil, a very fiend.

TRANIO: Why, she's a devil, a devil, the devil's dam.

GREMIO: Tut! she's a lamb, a dove, a fool to him.

I'll tell you, Sir Lucentio: when the priest

Should ask, if Katherine should be his wife,

'Ay, by goggs woones!' Quoth he; and swore so loud

That, all amaz'd, the priest let fall the book

And , as he stoop'd again to take it up

This mad-brain'd bridegroom took him such a cuff

That down fell priest and book and book and priest.

'Now, take them up,' quoth he, 'if any list.'

(Music plays.)

(Enter PETRUCHIO, KATHERINE, BIANCA, BAPTISTA, HORTENSIO with GRUMIO and train.)

PETRUCHIO: Gentlemen and friends, I thank you for your pains.

I know you think to dine with me today

And have prepar'd great store of wedding cheer,

But so it is, my haste doth call me hence

And therefore here I mean to take my leave.

BAPTISTA: Is't possible you will away tonight?

PETRUCHIO: I must away today, before night come.

Make it no wonder; if you knew my business,

You would entreat me rather go than stay.

And, honest company, I thank you all,

That have beheld me give away myself

To this most patient, sweet, and virtuous wife.

Dine with my father, drink a health to me,

For I must hence; and farewell to you all.

TRANIO: Let us entreat you stay till after dinner.

PETRUCHIO: It may not be.

GREMIO: Let me entreat you.

PETRUCHIO: It cannot be.

KATHERINA: Let me entreat you.

PETRUCHIO: I am content.

KATHERINA: Are you content to stay?

PETRUCHIO: I am content you shall entreat me stay,

But yet not stay, entreat me how you can.

KATHERINA: Now if you love me, stay.

PETRUCHIO: Grumio, my horse!

GRUMIO: Ay, sir, they be ready; the oats have eaten the horses.

KATHERINA: Nay then,

Do what thou canst, I will not go today;

No, nor tomorrow, not till I please myself.

The door is open, sir, there lies your way;

You may be jogging while your boots are green;

For me, I'll not be gone till I please myself.

'Tis like you'll prove a jolly surly groom,

That take it on you at the first so roundly.

PETRUCHIO: O Kate! content thee; prethee, be not angry.

KATHERINA: I will be angry; what hast thou to do?

Father, be quiet; he shall stay my leisure.

GREMIO: Ay, marry, sir, now it begins to work.

KATHERINA: Gentlemen, forward to the bridal dinner:

I see a woman may be made a fool

If she had not a spirit to resist.

PETRUCHIO: They shall go forward, Kate, at thy command.

Obey the bride, you that attend on her;

Go to the feast, revel and domineer,

Carouse full measure to her maidenhead,

Be mad and merry, or go hang yourselves;

But for my bonny Kate, she must with me.

Nay, look not big, not stamp, nor stare, nor fret;

I will be master of what is mine own.

She is my goods, my chattels; she is my house,

My household stuff, my field, my barn,

My horse, my ox, my ass, my anything;

And here she stands, touch her whoever dare;

I'll bring mine action on the proudest he

That stops my way in Padua. Grumio,

Draw forth thy weapon, we are beset with thieves;

Rescue they mistress, if thou be a man.

Fear not, sweet wench; they shall not touch thee, Kate:

I'll buckler thee against a million.

(Exeunt PETRUCHIO, KATHERINA, and GRUMIO.)

BAPTISTA: Nay, let them go, a couple of quiet ones.

GREMIO: Went they not quickly I should die with laughing.

TRANIO: Of all made matches never was the like.

LUCENTIO: Mistress, what's your opinion of your sister?

BIANCA: That being mad herself, she's madly mated.

GREMIO: I warrant him, Petruchio is Kated.

BAPTISTA: Neighbors and friends, though bride and bridegroom wants

For to supply the places at the table,

You know there wants no junkets at the feast.

Lucentio, you shall supply the bridegroom's place,

And let Bianca take her sister's room.

TRANIO: Shall sweet Bianca practice how to bride it?

BAPTISTA: She shall, Lucentio. Come, gentlemen, let's go.

(Exeunt.)

ACT III SCENE III

(Enter GRUMIO, CURTIS and four or five SERVINGMEN.)

NATHANIEL: All things is ready. How near is our master?

GRUMIO: E'en at hand, alighted by this; and therefore be not -- Cock's passion, silence! I hear my master.

(Enter PETRUCHIO and KATE.)

PETRUCHIO: Where be these knaves? What! no man at door

To hold my stirrup nor to take my horse?

Where is Nathaniel, Gregory, Philip? --

ALL SERVINGMEN: Here, here, sir; here, sir.

PETRUCHIO: Here, sir! here, sir! here, sir! here, sir!

You loggerheaded and unpolish'd grooms!

What, no attendance? no regard? no duty?

Where is the foolish knave I sent before?

GRUMIO: Here, sir; as foolish as I was before.

PETRUCHIO: You peasant swain! you whoreson malt-horse drudge!

Did I not bid thee meet me in the park

And bring along these rascal knaves with thee.

GRUMIO: Nathaniel's coat, sir, was not fully made

And Gabrel's pumps were all unpink'd I' th' heel;

There was no link to color Peter's hat

And Walter's dagger was not come from sheathing;

There were none fine but Adam, Rafe, and Gregory;

The rest were ragged, old, and beggarly.

Yet, as they are, here are they come to meet you.

PETRUCHIO: Go, rascals, go, and fetch my supper in.

(Exeunt SERVANTS.)

'Where is the life that late I led?'

Where are those -- ? Sit down, Kate, and welcome.

Food, food, food, food!

(Enter SERVANTS with supper.)

Why, when, I say? -- Nay, good sweet Kate, be merry. --

Off with my boots, you rogues! you villains! When?

'It was the friar of orders grey,

As he forth walked on his way':

Out, you rogue! you pluck my foot awry;

Take that, and mend the plucking of the other.

(Strikes him.)

Be merry, Kate. Some water, here; what, ho!

(Enter one with water.)

Where's my spaniel Troilus? Sirrah, get you hence

And bid my cousin Ferdinand come hither: *(Exit Servant.)*

One, Kate, that you must kiss and be acquainted with.

Where are my slippers? Shall I have some water?

Come, Kate, and wash, and welcome heartily. --

You whoreson villain! will you let it fall? *(Strikes him.)*

KATHERINA: Patience, I pray you; 'twas a fault unwilling.

PETRUCHIO: A whoreson, beetle-headed, flap-ear'd knave!

Come, Kate, sit down; I know you have a stomach.

Will you give thanks, sweet Kate, or else shall I? --

What's this? mutton?

1 SERVINGMAN: Ay.

PETRUCHIO: Who brought it?

PETER: I.

PETRUCHIO: 'Tis burnt; and so is all the meat.

What dogs are these! Where is the rascal cook?

How durst you, villains, bring it from the dresser,

And serve it thus to me that love it not?

(Throws the meat about the stage.)

There, take it to you, trenchers, cups, and all.

You heedless joltheads and unmanner'd slaves!

What, do you grumble? I'll be with you straight.

KATHERINA: I pray you, husband, be not so disquiet:

The meat was well if you were so contented.

PETRUCHIO: I tell thee, Kate, 'twas burnt and dried sway

And I expressly am forbid to touch it,

For it engenders choler, planteth anger,

And better 'twere that both of us did fast,

Since, of ourselves, ourselves are choleric,

Than feed it with such overroasted flesh.

Be patient; tomorrow't shall be mended,

And for this night we'll fast for company.

Come, I will bring thee to thy bridal chamber.

(Exeunt.)

(Enter Servants severally.)

NATHANIEL: Peter, didst ever see the like?

PETER: He kills her in her own humor.

(Enter Curtis, a Servant.)

GRUMIO: Where is he?

CURTIS: In her chamber, making a sermon of continency to her:

And rails and swears and rates, that she, poor soul,

And sits as one new-risen from a dream.

Away, away! For he is coming hither. *(Exeunt.)*

(Enter PETRUCHIO.)

PETRUCHIO: Thus have I politicly begun my reign

And 'tis my hope to end successfully.

My falcon now is sharp and passing empty

And till she stoop she must not be full gorg'd,

For then she never looks upon her lure.

Another way I have to man my haggard,

To make her come and know her keeper's call;

That bate and beat and will not be obedient.

She eat no meat today, nor none shall eat;

Last night she slept not, nor tonight she shall not:

As with the meat, some underserved fault

I'll find about the making of the bed

And here I'll fling the pillow, there the bolster,

This way the coverlet, another way the sheets.

Ay, and amid this hurly I intend

That all is done in reverend care of her,

And in conclusion she shall watch all night;

And with the clamor keep her still awake.

This is the way to kill a wife with kindness,

And thus I'll curb her mad and headstrong humor.

He that knows better how to tame a shrew,

Now let him speak: 'tis charity to shrew. *(Exit.)*

ACT III SCENE IV

(Enter PEDANT, TRANIO, and BIONDELLO.)

PEDANT: God save you, sir!

TRANIO: And you, sir! you are welcome.

Travel you far on, or are you at the farthest?

PEDANT: Sir, at the farthest for a week or two,

But then up farther and as far as Rome;

And so to Tripoli if God lend me life.

TRANIO: First, tell me, have you ever been at Pisa?

PEDANT: Ay, sir, in Pisa have I often ben;

Pisa, renowned for grave citizens.

TRANIO: Among them, know you one Vincentio?

PEDANT: I know him not but I have heard of him;

A merchant of incomparable wealth.

TRANIO: He is my father, sir; and, sooth to say,

In count'nance somewhat doth resemble you.

BIONDELLO: *(Aside.)* As much as an apple doth an oyster, and all one.

TRANIO: To save your life in this extremity

This favor will I do for his sake,

And think it not the worst of all your fortunes

That you are like to Sir Vincentio.

His name and credit shall you undertake

And in my house you shall be friendly lodg'd.

Look that you take upon you as you should!

You understand me, sir; so shall you stay

Till you have done your business in the city.

If this be court'sy, sir, accept of it.

PEDANT: O sir, I do; and will repute you ever

The patron of my life and liberty.

TRANIO: Then go with me to make the matter good.

This, by the way, I let you understand:

My father is here look'd for every day

To pass assurance of a dower in marriage

'Twixt me and one Baptista's daughter here.

In all these circumstances I'll instruct you.

Go with me to clothe you as becomes you.

(Exeunt.)

ACT IV SCENE I

(Enter KATHERINA and GRUMIO.)

GRUMIO: No, no, forsooth; I dare not for my life.

KATHERINA: The more my wrong, the more his spite appears.

What, did he marry me to famish me?

Beggars, that come unto my father's door,

Upon entreaty have a present alms;

If not, elsewhere they meet with charity.

But I, who never knew how to entreat

Nor never needed that I should entreat,

Am starv'd for meat, giddy for lack of sleep,

With oaths kept waking and with brawling fed.

And that which spites me more than all these wants,

He does it under name of perfect love,

As who should say, if I should sleep or eat

'Twere deadly sickness or else present death.

I prithee go and get me some repast;

I care not what, so it be wholesome food.

GRUMIO: What say you to a neat's foot?

KATHERINA: 'Tis passing good: I prethee let me have it.

GRUMIO: I fear it is too choleric a meat.

How say you to a fat tripe finely broil'd?

KATHERINA: I like it well: good Grumio, fetch it me.

GRUMIO: I cannot tell; I fear 'tis choleric.

What say you to a piece of beef and mustard?

KATHERINA: A dish that I do love to feed upon.

GRUMIO: Ay, but the mustard is too hot a little.

KATHERINA: Why then, the beef, and let the mustard rest.

GRUMIO: Nay then, I will not; you shall have the mustard

Or else you get no beef of Grumio.

KATHERINA: Then both or one, or anything thou wilt.

GRUMIO: Why then, the mustard without the beef.

KATHERINA: Go, get thee gone, thou false deluding

Slave, *(Beats him.)*

That feed'st me with the very name of meat.

Sorrow on thee and all pack of you

That triumph thus upon my misery!

Go, get thee gone, I say.

(Enter PETRUCHIO, and HORTENSIO with meat.)

PETRUCHIO: How fares my Kate? What, sweeting, all amort?

HORTENSIO: Mistress, what cheer?

KATHERINA: Faith, as cold as can be.

PETRUCHIO: Pluck up thy spirits; look cheerfully upon me.

Here, love; thou seest how diligent I am

To dress thy meat myself and bring it thee.

I am sure, sweet Kate, this kindness merits thanks.

What! not a word? Nay then, thou lov'st it not

And all my pains is sorted to no proof.

Here, take away this dish.

KATHERINA: I pray you, let it stand.

PETRUCHIO: The poorest service is repaid with thanks

And so shall mine, before you touch the meat.

KATHERINA: I thank you, sir.

HORTENSIO: Signior Petruchio, fie! you are to blame.

Come, Mistress Kate, I'll bear you company.

PETRUCHIO: Eat it up all, Hortensio, if thou lov'st me,

Much good do it unto thy gentle heart!

Kate, eat apace. And now, my honey love,

Will we return unto thy father's house

And revel it as bravely as the best,

With silken coats and caps and golden rings,

With ruffs and cuffs and fardingales and things;

With scarfs and fans and double change of brav'ry,

With amber bracelets, beads, and all this knav'ry.

What! hast thou din'd? The tailor stays thy leisure

To deck thy body with his ruffling treasure.

(Enter TAILOR.)

Come, tailor, let us see these ornaments;

Lay forth the gown. --

(Enter HABERDASHER.)

What news with you, sir?

HABERDASHER: Here is the cap your worship did bespeak.

PETRUCHIO: Why, this was molded on a porringer;

A velvet dish: fie, fie! 'tis lewd and filthy:

Why, 'tis a cockle or a walnut shell,

A knack, a toy, a trick, a baby's cap --

Away with it! come, let me have a bigger.

KATHERINA: I'll have no bigger, this doth fit the time

And gentlewomen wear such caps as these.

PETRUCHIO: When you are gentle you shall have one too --

And not till then.

HORTENSIO: *(Aside.)* That will not be in haste.

KATHERINA: Why, sir, I trust I may have leave to speak,

And speak I will; I am no child, no babe.

Your betters have endur'd me say my mind

And if you cannot, best you stop your ears.

My tongue will tell the anger of my heart

Or else my heart, concealing it, will break,

And rather than it shall I will be free

Even to the uttermost, as I please, in words.

PETRUCHIO: Why, thou sayst true; it is a paltry cap,

A custard-coffin, a bauble, a silken pie.

I love thee well in that thou lik'st it not.

KATHERINA: Love me or love me not, I like the cap

And I will have or I will have none. *(Exit HABERDASHER.)*

PETRUCHIO: Thy gown? why, ay: come, tailor, let us see't.

O mercy, God! what masquing stuff is here?

What's this? a sleeve? 'tis like a demi-cannon.

What! up and down, carv'd like an apple tart?

Here's a snip and nip and cut and slish and slash,

Like to a censer in a barber's shop.

Why, what, a devil's name, tailor, call'st thou this?

HORTENSIO: *(Aside.)* I see, she's like to have neither cap nor gown.

TAILOR: You bid me make it orderly and well,

According to the fashion and the time.

PETRUCHIO: Marry, and did; but if you be rememb'red,

I did not bid you mar it to the time.

KATHERINA: I never saw a better-fashion'd gown,

More quaint, more pleasing, nor more commendable.

Belike you mean to make a puppet of me.

PETRUCHIO: Why, true; he means to make a puppet of thee.

TAILOR: She says your worship means to make a puppet of her.

PETRUCHIO: O monstrous arrogance!

Thou liest, thou thread, thou thimble,

Thou yard, three-quarters, half yard, quarter, nail!

Thou flea, thou nit, thou winter-cricket thou!

Brav'd in mine own house with a skein of thread!

Away! thou rag, thou quantity, thou remnant,

Or I shall so bemete thee with thy yard

As thou shalt think on prating whilst thou liv'st!

I tell thee, I, that thou hast marr'd her gown.

Well, sir, in brief, the gown is not for me.

GRUMIO: You are in the right, sir; 'tis for my mistress.

PETRUCHIO: Go, take it up unto thy master's use.

GRUMIO: Villain, not for thy life!

Take up my mistress' gown to his master's use!

O, fie, fie, fie!

PETRUCHIO: *(Aside.)* Hortensio, say thou wilt see the tailor paid.

Go take it hence; be gone and say no more.

HORTENSIO: Tailor, I'll pay thee for thy gown tomorrow;

Take no unkindness of his hasty words.

Away! I say; commend me to thy master. *(Exit TAILOR.)*

PETRUCHIO: Well, come, my Kate; we will unto your father's,

Even in these honest mean habiliments.

Our purses shall be proud, our garments poor,

For 'tis the mind that makes the body rich;

And as the sun breaks through the darkest clouds

So honor peereth in the meanest habit.

What, is the jay more precious than the lark

Because his feathers are more beautiful?

Or is the adder better than the eel

Because his painted skin contents the eye?

O no, good Kate; neither art thou the worse

For this poor furniture and mean array.

If thou account'st it shame, lay it on me

And therefore frolic; we will hence forthwith

To feast and sport us at thy father's house.

Go call my men, and let us straight to him;

And bring our horses unto Long-lane end;

There will we mount, and thither walk on foot.

Let's see; I think 'tis now some seen o'clock

And well we may come there by dinnertime.

KATHERINE: I dare assure you, sir, 'tis almost two

And 'twill be suppertime ere you come there.

PETRUCHIO: It shall be seven ere I go to horse.

Look, what I speak or do or think to do,

You are still crossing it. Sirs, let't alone:

I will not go today; and ere I do,

It shall be what o'clock I say it is.

HORTENSIO: Why, so this gallant will command the sun.

(Exeunt.)

ACT IV SCENE III

(Enter PETRUCHIO, KATHERINA, HORTENSIO with Servants.)

PETRUCHIO: Come on, a God's name; once more toward our father's.

Good Lord, how bright and goodly shines the moon!

KATHERINA: The moon! the sun: it is not moonlight now.

PETRUCHIO: I say it is the moon that shines so bright.

KATHERINA: I know that it is the sun that shines so bright.

PETRUCHIO: Now, by my mother's son, and that's myself,

It shall be moon or star or what I list,

Or ere I journey to your father's house.

Go on and fetch our horses back again.

Evermore cross'd and cross'd; nothing but cross'd!

HORTENSIO: Say as he says or we shall never go.

KATHERINA: Forward, I pray, since we have come so far,

And be it moon or sun or what you please.

And if you please to call it a rush-candle,

Henceforth I vow it shall be so for me.

PETRUCHIO: I say it is the moon.

KATHERINA: I know it is the moon.

PETRUCHIO: Nay, then you lie; it is the blessed sun.

KATHERINA: Then God be bless'd, it is the blessed sun!

But sun it is not when you say it is not,

And the moon changes even as your mind.

What you will have it nam'd, even that it is;

And so it shall be so for Katherine.

HORTENSIO: Petruchio, go thy ways; the field is won.

PETRUCHIO: Well, forward, forward! thus the bowl should run

And not unluckily against the bias.

But soft! company is coming here.

(Enter VINCENTIO.)

(To VINCENTIO.) Good morrow, gentle mistress: where away?

Tell me, sweet Kate, and tell me truly too,

Hast though beheld a fresher gentlewoman?

Such war of white and red within her cheeks!

What stars do spangle heaven with such beauty

As those two eyes become that heavenly face?

Fair lovely maid, once more good day to thee.

Sweet Kate, embrace her for her beauty's sake.

KATHERINA: Young budding virgin, fair and fresh and sweet,

Whether away, or where is thy abode?

PETRUCHIO: Why, how now, Kate! I hope thou art not mad;

This is a man, old, wrinkled, faded, wither'd,

And not a maiden, as thou sayst he is.

KATHERINA: Pardon, old father, my mistaking eyes

That have been so bedazzled with the sun

That everything I look on seemeth green.

Now I perceive thou art a reverent father;

Pardon, I pray thee, for my mad mistaking.

PETRUCHIO: Do, good old grandsire; and withal make known.

Which way thou travellest: if along with us,

We shall be joyful of thy company.

VINCENTIO: Fair sir, and you my merry mistress,

That with your strange encounter much amaz'd me,

My name is called Vincentio; my dwelling, Pisa;

And bound I am to Padua, there to visit

A son of mine, which long I have not seen.

PETRUCHIO: What is his name?

VINCENTIO: Lucentio, gentle sir.

PETRUCHIO: Happily met; the happier for thy son.

And now by law, as well as reverent age,

I may entitle thee my loving father:

The sister to my wife, this gentlewoman,

They son by this hath married. Wonder not

Nor be not griev'd: she is of good esteem,

Her dowry wealthy, and of worthy birth;

Beside, so qualified as may beseem

The spouse of any noble gentleman.

Let me embrace with old Vincentio

And wander we to see thy honest son,

Who will of thy arrival be full joyous.

VINCENTIO: But is this true? or is it else your pleasure,

Like pleasant travelers, to break a jest

Upon the company you overtake?

HORTENSIO: I do assure thee, father, so it is.

PETRUCHIO: Come, go along, and see the truth herof;

For our first merriment hath made thee jealous.

(Exeunt.)

ACT IV SCENE IV

(Enter BIONDELLO, LUCENTIO, BIANCA; GREMIO is out before.)

BIONDELLO: Softly and swiftly, sir, for the priest is ready.

LUCENTIO: I fly, Biondello, but they may chance to need thee at home; therefore leave us.

(Exit with BIANCA.)

BIONDELLO: Nay, faith, I'll see the church a your back; and then come back to my master's as

soon as I can. (Exit.)

(Enter PETRUCHIO, KATE, VINCENTIO, and GRUMIO with Attendants.)

PETRUCHIO: Sir, here's the door, this is Lucentio's house:

My father's bears more toward the market place;

Thither must I and here I leave you, sir.

VINCENTIO: You shall not choose but drink before you go.

I think I shall command your welcome here

And, by all likelihood, some cheer is toward. *(Knock.)*

GREMIO: They're busy within; you were best knock louder.

(PEDANT looks out of the window.)

PEDANT: What's he that knocks as he would beat down the gate?

VINCENTIO: Is Signior Lucentio within, sir?

PEDANT: He's within, sir, but not to be spoken withal.

PETRUCHIO: Nay, I told you your son was well beloved in Padua. Do you hear, sir? To leave frivoulous circumstances, I pray you tell Signior Lucentio that his father is come from Pisa and is here at the door to speak with him.

PEDANT: Thou liest; his father is come from Padua and here looking out the window.

VINCENTIO: Art thou his father?

PEDANT: Ay sir, so his mother says, if I may believe her.

PETRUCHIO: *(To VINCENTIO.)* Why how now, gentleman! why this is flat knavery, to take upon you another man's name.

PEDANT: Lay hands on the villain; I believe, a means to cozen somebody in this city under my countenance.

(Enter BIONDELLO.)

BIONDELLO: I have seen them in the church together; God send 'em good shipping! But who is here? mine old master, Vincentio! now we are undone and brought to nothing.

VINCENTIO: Come hither, you rogue. What, have you forgot me?

BIONDELLO: Forgot you! no sir. I could not forget you, for I never saw you before in all my life.

VINCENTIO: What, you notorious villain! didst thou never see thy master's father, Vincentio?

BIONDELLO: What, my old worshipful old master? yes, marry, sir: see where he looks out of the window.

VINCENTIO: Is't so, indeed? *(He beats BIONDELLO.)*

BIONDELLO: Help, help, help! here's a madman will murder me. *(Exit.)*

PEDANT: Help, son! help, Signior Baptista! *(Exit from above.)*

PETRUCHIO: Prithee, Kate, let's stand aside and see the end of this controversy.

(They retire.)

(Enter PEDANT below with Servants, BAPTISTA, and TRANIO.)

TRANIO: Sir, what are you that offer to beat my servant?

VINCENTIO: What am I, sir! nay, what are you, sir?

O immortal gods! O fine villain! A silken doublet! a velvet hose! a scarlet cloak! and a copatain hat! O, I am undone! I am undone! while I play the good husband at home, my son and my servant spend all at the university.

TRANIO: How now! what's the matter?

BAPTISTA: What, is the man lunatic?

TRANIO: Sir, you seem a sober ancient gentleman by your habit, but your words show you a madman. Why sir, what cerns it you if I wear pearl and gold? I thank my good father, I am able to maintain it.

VINCENTIO: Thy father! O villain! he is a sailmaker in Bergamo.

BAPTISTA: You mistake, sir, you mistake, sir. Pray, what do you think is his name?

VINCENTIO: His name! as if I knew not his name! I have brought him up ever since he was three years old, and his name is Tranio.

PEDANT: Away, away, mad ass! his name is Lucentio and he is mine only son, and heir to the lands of me, Signoir Vincentio.

VINCENTIO: Lucentio! O he hath murd'red his master.

Lay hold on him, I charge you in the duke's name. O my son! tell me, thou villain, where is my son Lucentio?

TRANIO: Call forth an officer.

(Enter one with an officer.)

Carry this mad knave to the jail. Father Baptista, I charge you wee that he be forthcoming.

VINCENTIO: Carry me to the jail!

GREMIO: Stay, officer: he shall not go to prison.

BAPTISTA: Talk not, Signior Gremio. I say he shall go to prison.

GREMIO: Take heed, Signior Baptista, lest you be cony-catched in this business. I dare swear this is the right Vincentio.

PEDANT: Swear, if thou dar'st.

GREMIO: Nay, I dare not swear it.

TRANIO: Then thou wert best say that I am not Lucentio.

GREMIO: Yes, I know thee to be Signior Lucentio.

BAPTISTA: Away with the dotard; to the jail with him!

VINCENTIO: Thus strangers may be hal'd and abused;

O monstrous villain!

(Enter BIONDELLO, LUCENTIO, and BIANCA.)

BIONDELLO: O we are spoil'd; and yonder he is: deny him, forswear him, or else we are all undone.

(Exeunt BIONDELLO, TRANIO, and PEDANT as fast as may be.)

LUCENTIO: Pardon, sweet father. *(Kneel.)*

VINCENTIO: Lives my sweet son?

BIANCA: Pardon, dear father.

BAPTISTA: How hast thou offended?

Where is Lucentio?

LUCENTIO: Here's Lucentio,

Right son to the right Vincentio,

That have by marriage made thy daughter mine

While counterfeit supposes blear'd thine eyne.

GREMIO: Here's packing, with a witness, to deceive us all!

VINCENTIO: Where is that damned villain Tranio

That fac'd and brav'd me in this matter so?

BAPTISTA: Why, tell me, is not this my Cambio?

BIANCA: Cambio is chang'd into Lucentio.

LUCENTIO: Love wrought these miracles. Bianca's love

Made me exchange my state with Tranio

While he did bear my countenance in the town,

And happily I have arriv'd at the last

Unto the wished haven of my bliss.

What Tranio did, myself enforc'd him to;

Then pardon him, sweet father, for my sake.

VINCENTIO: I'll slit the villain's nose, that would have sent me to the jail.

BAPTISTA: But do you hear, sir? Have you married my daughter without asking my good will?

VINCENTIO: Fear not, Baptista; we will content you, go to: but I will in, to be revenged for

this villainy. *(Exit.)*

BAPTISTA: And I, to sound the depth of this knavery. *(Exit.)*

LUCENTIO: Look not pale, Bianca; thy father will not frown. *(Exeunt LUCENTIO and BIANCA.)*

GREMIO: My cake is dough, but I'll in among the rest

Out of hope of all but my share of the feast. *(Exit.)*

KATHERINA: Husband, let's follow, to see the end of this ado.

PETRUCHIO: First kiss me, Kate, and we will.

KATHERINA: What! in the midst of the street?

PETRUCHIO: What! art thou asham'd of me?

KATHERINA: No sir, god forbid; but asham'd to kiss.

PETRUCHIO: Why, then let's home again. Come sirrah, let's away.

KATHERINA: Nay, I will give thee a kiss; now pray thee, love, stay.

PETRUCHIO: Is not this well?: Come, my sweet Kate;

Better once than never, for never too late. *(Exeunt.)*

ACT V SCENE I

(Enter BAPTISTA, VINCENTIO, GREMIO, PEDANT, LUCENTIO, and BIANCA, TRANIO, BIONDELLO,

GRUMIO, PETRUCHIO, KATHERINA, HORTENSIO, and WIDOW, the Servingmen with TRANIO

bringing in a banquet.)

LUCENTIO: At last, though long, our jarring notes agree;

And time it is, when raging war is done,

To smile at scapes and perils overblown.

My fair Bianca, bid my father welcome

While I with self-same kindness welcome thine.

Brother Petruchio, sister Katherina,

And thou, Hortensio, with thy loving widow,

Feast with the best and welcome to my house;

My banker is to close our stomachs up

After our great good cheer. Pray you, sit down;

For now we sit to chat as well as eat.

PETRUCHIO: Nothing but sit and sit, and eat and eat!

BAPTISTA: Padua affords this kindness, son Petruchio.

PETRUCHIO: Padua affords nothing but what is kind.

(Exit BIANCA, with KATHERINA and WIDOW.)

BAPTISTA: Now, in good sadness, son Petruchio,

I think thou hast the veriest shrew of all.

PETRUCHIO: Well, I say no: and therefore, for assurance,

Let's each one send unto his wife,

And he whose wife is most obedient

To come at first when he doth send for her

Shall win the wager which we will propose.

HORTENSIO: Content. What's the wager?

LUCENTIO: Twenty crowns.

PETRUCHIO: Twenty crowns!

I'll venture so much of my hawk or hound,

But twenty time so much upon my wife.

LUCENTIO: A hundred then.

HORTENSIO: Content.

PETRUCHIO: A match! 'tis done.

HORTENSIO: Who shall begin?

LUCENTIO: That will I.

Go Biondello, bid your mistress come to me.

BIONDELLO: I go. *(Exit.)*

BAPTISTA: Son, I'll be your half, Bianca comes.

LUCENTIO: I'll have no halves; I'll bear it all myself.

(Enter BIONDELLO.)

How how! what news?

BIONDELLO: Sir, my mistress sends you word

That she is busy and she cannot come.

PETRUCHIO: How! she is busy and she cannot come!

Is that an answer?

GREMIO: Ay, and a kind one too;

Pray God, sir, your wife send you not a worse.

PETRUCHIO: I hope, better.

HORTENSIO: Sirrah Biondello, go and entreat my wife

To come to me forthwith. *(Exit BIONDELLO.)*

PETRUCHIO: O ho! entreat her!

Nay, then she must needs come.

HORTENSIO: I am afraid, sir,

Do what you can, yours will not be entreated.

(Enter BIONDELLO.)

Now where's my wife?

BIONDELLO: She says you have some goodly jest in hand.

She will not come; she bids you come to her.

PETRUCHIO: Worse and worse; she will not come! O vilde,

Intolerable, not to be endur'd!

Sirrah Grumio, go to your mistress; say

I command her come to me.

(Exit GRUMIO.)

HORTENSIO: I know her answer.

PETRUCHIO: What?

HORTENSIO: She will not.

PETRUCHIO: The fouler fortune mine, and there an end.

(Enter KATHERINA.)

BAPTISTA: Now, by my hollidam, here comes Katherina!

KATHERINA: What is your will, sir, that you send for me?

PETRUCHIO: Where is your sister, and Hortensio's wife?

KATHERINA: They sit conferring by the parlor fire.

PETRUCHIO: Go fetch them hither; if they deny to come,

Swinge me them soundly forth unto their husbands.

Away, I say, and bring them hither straight.

(Exit KATHERINA.)

LUCENTIO: Here is a wonder, if you talk of a wonder.

HORTENSIO: And so it is. I wonder what it bodes.

PETRUCHIO: Marry, peace it bodes, and love, and quiet life,

An awful rule and right supremacy;

And, to be short, what not that's sweet and happy.

BAPTISTA: Now fair befall thee, good Petruchio!

The wager thou hast won and I will add

Unto their losses twenty thousand crowns,

Another dowry to another daughter,

For she is chang'd, as she had never been.

PETRUCHIO: Nay, I will win my wager better yet

And show more sign of her obedience,

Her new-built virtue and obedience.

(Enter KATE, BIANCA, and WIDOW.)

See where she comes and brings your froward wives

As prisoners to her womanly persuasion.

Katerine, that cap of yours becomes you not:

Off with that bauble, throw it under foot.

WIDOW: Lord! let me never have a cause to sigh

Till I be brought to such a silly pass!

BIANCA: Fie! what a foolish duty call you this?

LUCENTIO: I would your duty were as foolish too;

The wisdom of your duty, fair Bianca,

Hath cost me five hundred crowns since suppertime.

BIANCA: The more fool you are for laying on my duty.

PETRUCHIO: Katherine, I charge thee, tell these headstrong women

What duty they do owe their lords and husbands.

WIDOW: Come, come you're mocking; we will have no telling.

PETRUCHIO: Come on, I say; and first begin with her.

WIDOW: She shall not.

PETRUCHIO: I say she shall: and first begin with her.

KATHERINA: Fie, fie! unknit that threat'ning unkind brow

And dart not scornful glances from those eyes

To wound thy lord, thy king, thy governor.

It blots thy beauty as frosts do bite the meads,

Confounds thy fame as whirlwinds shake fair buds,

And in no sense is meet or amiable.

A woman mov'd is like a fountain troubled,

Muddy, ill-seeming, thick, bereft of beauty;

And while it is so, none so dry or thirsty

Will deign to sip or touch one drop of it.

Thy husband is thy lord, thy life, thy keeper,

Thy head, thy sovereign; one that cares for thee,

And for they maintenance commits his body

To painful labor both by sea and land,

To watch the night in storms, the day in cold,

Whilst thou li'st warm at home, secure and safe;

And craves no other tribute at thy hands

But love, fair looks, and true obedience;

Too little payment for so great a debt.

Such duty as the subject owes the prince,

Even such a woman oweth to her husband;

And when she is froward, peevish, sullen, sour,

And not obedient to his honest will,

What is she but a foul contending rebel

And graceless traitor to her loving lord? --

I am asham'd that women are so simple

To offer war where they should kneel for peace,

Or seek for rule, supremacy, and sway,

When they are bound to serve, love, and obey.

Why are our bodies soft and weak and smooth,

Unapt to toil and trouble in the world,

But that our soft conditions and our hearts

Should well agree with our external parts?

Come, come, you forward and unable worms!

My mind hath been as big as one of yours,

My heart as great, my reason haply more,

To bandy word for word and frown for frown;

But now I see our lances are but straws,

Our strength as weak, our weakness past compare,

That seeming to be most which we indeed least are.

Then vail your stomachs, for it is no boot,

And place your hands below your husband's foot:

In token of which duty, if he please,

My hand is ready; may it do him ease.

PETRUCHIO: Why, there's a wench! Come on and kiss me, Kate.

LUCENTIO: Well, go thy ways, old lad, for thou shalt ha't.

VINCENTIO: 'Tis a good hearing when children are toward.

LUCENTIO: But a harsh hearing when women are froward.

PETRUCHIO: Come, Kate, we'll to bed.

We three are married, but you two are sped.

'Twas I won the wager, *(To Lucentio.)* though you hit the white;

And, being a winner, God gave you good night!

(Exit PETRUCHIO with KATHERINA.)

HORTENSIO: Now, go thy ways; thou hast tam'd a curst shrow.

LUCENTIO: 'Tis a wonder, by your leave, she will be tam'd so.

(Exeunt.) (Curtain.)

Printed in Great Britain
by Amazon